# And God Cried, Too

# And God Cried, Too

## A Kid's Book of Healing and Hope

by Marc Gellman

*illustrations by Harry Bliss*

**HarperTrophy®**
*An Imprint of HarperCollinsPublishers*

HarperTrophy® is a registered trademark of HarperCollins Publishers Inc.

And God Cried, Too
Text copyright © 2002 by Marc Gellman
Illustrations copyright © 2002 by Harry Bliss
Printed in the United States of America.
For information address
HarperCollins Children's Books,
a division of HarperCollins Publishers,
1350 Avenue of the Americas, New York, NY 10019.

Library of Congress Cataloging-in-Publication Data
Gellman, Marc.
And God cried, too : a kid's book of healing and hope / by Marc Gellman ;
illustrations by Harry Bliss.— 1st ed.
    p.   cm.
Summary: The angel Gabriel helps Mikey, a guardian-angel-in-training, to
understand why bad things happen for what seems to be no reason, and how
to hold on to hope and faith during difficult times.
ISBN 0-06-009886-4 (pbk.) — ISBN 0-06-009887-2 (lib. bdg.)
1. Consolation—Juvenile literature.   2. Suffering—Religious aspects—
Juvenile literature. [1. Consolation.   2. Fairness.   3. Justice.   4. Hope.
5. Faith.   6. Conduct of life.]   I. Bliss, Harry, 1964– ill.   II. Title.
BL65.S85 .G45 2002                                          2002005645
291.2'118—dc21                                                      CIP
                                                                     AC

Typography by Hilary Zarycky
❖
First Harper Trophy edition, 2002
Visit us on the World Wide Web!
www.harperchildrens.com

*For Moochie . . .*
*my daughter,*
*my muse*

# Contents

# Things for Adults to Think About First . . .

*This is a book for children, but it's also a book for adults who aren't sure how to bring hope to children who are sad or scared. All kids deal with loss on some level, and helping them deal with the resulting feelings of anger, sadness, and fear is an important part of every parent's job.*

*This book is about big issues that most adults think are just too complicated and daunting for children to understand. I disagree strongly.*

*Children have a natural curiosity and a natural faith that is going to erupt when you least expect it. And the next thing you know, you are being asked if you think God is fair, or what happens to us after we die, or why God doesn't stop the bad things in the world. Then you must be a teacher and a source of hope and healing. So if you need a little extra help figuring out what to say, I hope this book is worthy of your child's questions.*

I chose to present the big questions in the form of stories about two angels. One is a little guardian-angel-in-training named Mikey who is asking some tough questions. His teacher is a chief angel named Gabe. In each chapter Gabe teaches Mikey something really important about life and loss. I hope the chapters work not only as stories but also as stories with a moral meaning.

At the end of each chapter I have included a section called "Things to think about. . . ." This is my way of speaking to your child in my own voice and clarifying the lessons of each Gabe and Mikey story. This is also my chance to offer my own encouragement and support for the spiritual curiosity of your child. Optimism is a learned skill, not just an attribute like being left-handed. I love to teach hope because my audience of children is already naturally hopeful. My job is to say in every different way I can think up, "Don't worry. Everything will be okay." I am happy to say it because I really do believe it.

This book is also about God. God is the source of hope and healing for me and for so many people. God carries us through the worst times and also *lifts us to joyousness in the best of times. I often give permission to children to be angry at God or to be patient while they find their way to God.*

*Many people believe in God but not in angels. Your child needs to know that I invented Gabe and Mikey, just as all storytellers invent their characters. Maybe there really are angels, and maybe two of them are even named Gabe and Mikey, but you don't have to believe in angels to believe in this book.*

*September 11, 2001, was a really scary time for kids. The fear and panic so many adults and children felt, and still feel, over this terrible tragedy inspired me to write this book. I hope it will help children answer questions that maybe before that day they'd never thought to ask.*

*Most of this book is not specifically about September 11, but all of it can be applied to September 11. The attack on America and its aftermath appear as a setting for several chapters. I felt that the best way to approach this event was indirectly, not head-on. It is just one more reason why our kids need hope and healing.*

*God bless!*

*Marc Gellman*

## Things for Kids to Think About First . . .

This is a book about the things that make us sad and the things that make us happy again. It's filled with stories about two angels. One is a little angel named Michael, but everyone in Heaven calls him Mikey. Mikey has lots of questions about how God runs the world. Maybe you've had some of the same questions, too. The other angel is a chief angel named Gabriel, but everybody calls him Gabe. Gabe is Mikey's teacher. Gabe is not a teacher like your teacher in school. He is a teacher the way your grandparents are teachers. He is old and wise and knows a lot about how the world works and God's part in all of it.

I hope you like the stories about Gabe and Mikey, but before you read them, maybe we should first talk about whether angels are real. Gabe and Mikey are not real. I know this because I made them up. I also made up the stories about them to help you feel better because maybe something bad happened in your life or maybe you have some of the same questions as Mikey. So if you don't believe in angels, that's okay. If you do believe in angels, that's okay too. I believe in angels because I think that God must need helpers to run the world. People can be God's helpers, which means that people can be angels too. But people don't have wings and a halo and fly around Heaven like angels. I just think God is happy to have all the helpers God can find.

God is also a part of this book. God does not say much in the book, but God is always around. I believe in God. Some of you may not believe in God, and that's okay. Whether you believe in God is something you have to figure out for yourself. You can't believe in God just because somebody tells you to.

Even though I am a grown-up, I get sad and scared just like you. I feel better when I talk to my family and my friends, but I also feel better when I pray to God and remember that God loves me and cares about me and is protecting me.

It has been a scary time for all of us since September 11, 2001. There are parts of this book *where Gabe and Mikey do things and learn things because of the attack on America on September 11, but the book is about every day, not just that day. This book is my way of trying to help you feel better after anything that has made you sad.*

*At the end of each chapter I put in a little section called "Things to think about. . . ." This is where I'm just talking to you, not telling you a made-up story. I give you some ideas to think about, but don't worry, there won't be a test. I just want you to think about big things, important things, things that really matter, and not just what color shirt you should wear today.*

*Well, that's pretty much it. Now it's time to introduce you to my made-up friends Gabe and Mikey, and their boss, who I do believe is real: God.*

*God bless you and . . . here we go.*

*Marc Gellman*

# And God Cried, Too

# 1

## Finding Mikey:

### What if nothing makes any sense?

Gabriel, the chief teaching angel, found this note taped to his office door in Heaven:

Dear Gabe,
  I quit. I know I could never become a
guardian angel because I get too upset

about what I see on earth. I see way too many terrible things happen to good people. It just doesn't make any sense. How can I explain God's ways to people when I don't understand God's ways myself? It all seems so unfair! I just don't understand how God is running things on earth. So I quit. Find yourself another angel who understands things better than I do.

Signed,

Michael (guardian-angel-in-training)

P.S. Everyone up here in Heaven calls me Mikey.

Gabriel spent the rest of the day flying around Heaven trying to find Mikey. Gabe had lost more than a few guardian-angels-in-training in his five thousand years of teaching. But he really did not want to lose Mikey, who had found his way into Gabe's heart.

After searching for most of the morning, Gabe finally spotted Mikey sleeping on a little cloud. He was all covered up by the cloud except that his nose stuck out of the top of the cloud and his wings stuck out of the bottom. Gabe woke him gently by brushing his own wing feathers under Mikey's nose and making him sneeze. *Ha-choo! Garumph!* And Mikey was up. He saw Gabe and tried to fly away as fast as he could.

Somewhere over the rainbow Gabe caught Mikey. Out of breath, Gabe said, "Look, I understand how you feel, but I don't want you to quit until you understand the way things really work, not just the way you *think* things work. Give me a chance to teach you, and give yourself a chance to learn a little more. Then, if you want to quit, you'll have my blessing. You are going to be a terrific guardian angel. You just don't know it yet."

"Leave me alone!" Mikey huffed.

"Okay," said Gabe sadly.

"Fine," said Mikey.

"Right. Then I guess it's good-bye," said Gabe.

"Yup! Good-bye," said Mikey.

"So long then," said Gabe.

"I'm gone!" said Mikey.

"That's what you said," said Gabe.

"Then I guess I'll just . . ." and at that moment, Mikey started to cry. He cried so hard, he soaked through his angel clothes and started a rainstorm under his cloud. Gabe flew close and held him and covered him with his two big wings like a feather blanket.

"It's just not fair. Things on earth don't make any sense. It's just so sad," sniffed Mikey.

"What God taught me," Gabe said softly, "and what I will teach you, my little angel, is not how to wipe away sadness and make everything happy again. What I will teach you cannot keep you from crying, but it will teach you how God makes sad and happy fit together down there on earth . . . and even up here in Heaven. It's amazing how God makes everything fit together perfectly, even though it might not look that way at first."

"Okay," said Mikey, drying his tears with his sleeve. "I'll give angel school another chance. I do want to understand how such a good God could allow so much bad to happen to good people. Okay, I'll try again."

"Good," said Gabe. "Come to my office tomorrow, and I will teach you your first earth lesson. And bring skis."

"Skis?" asked Mikey, puzzled.

"Skis," said Gabe.

"All right then, I'll see you tomorrow with . . ."

"Skis," they said together, laughing as they looped the loop back to the place in Heaven where the angels watch the sun set.

## Things to think about . . .

*Mikey wants the answers to some really big questions. How do the good and the bad parts of life fit together? Are the bad parts punishments for the bad stuff we do? Are the good parts rewards for the good we do? And why doesn't God stop the bad stuff?*

*Gabe can't just <u>tell</u> Mikey the answers. Life doesn't work that way. The answers to all the really big questions in life don't come through telling; they come through living. We learn the answers not by <u>hearing</u> the answers but by <u>living</u> our way into the answers. Because of what will happen in your life, you will live your way into your own big answers to your own big questions.*

*Please don't give up trying to answer your big questions, even if it takes time. Mikey almost quit because he was impatient. It's okay to want to quit.*

You've probably wanted to quit trying to answer those big questions, too. Stick it out. Keep trying. God believes in you and loves you. Nobody who loves you wants you to quit! And the cool thing is that you may just find your biggest and best answers the day after you almost quit.

And one last thing . . . if you can't exactly figure out how God is running the world, don't get frustrated or impatient. The way God runs the world is a big, gigantic mystery. Lots of people before you have thought about it for lots of years, and most of them have not figured it out. If you were trying to climb the tallest mountain, you wouldn't expect to climb it right away and without a long, tough struggle. Well, God made this mountain so it will be a big climb, but it will also be a wonderful climb and a great adventure. And what's more—you're not alone. Remember—God comes with you every step of the way, ready to catch you if you fall, comfort you when you're sad, help you find the right way through whatever you're going through. Let's get started. Mikey and Gabe are already way ahead of us.

# 2

## Hazards Exist That Are Not Marked:

### How can I go through life and not get hurt?

"It's freezing up here!" Mikey said to Gabe as they stood at the top of a ski run on a snowy mountain.

"I need to teach you something, and this is the best place to teach it," said Gabe. "Let's go. I'll meet you at the bottom of the mountain."

"Wait just one minute!" Mikey screamed. "This is a very big mountain, and I am a very small angel. Gabe, I'm a little scared. No, actually, I'm a lot scared!"

"Don't worry. To get down the mountain, you just have to ski fast enough to keep moving, but not so fast that you miss the signs. That's the first lesson. Now follow me and don't get lost. That's the second lesson."

Gabe shooshed down the mountain, with Mikey following close behind and yelling, "Ya-ha-hooey!" every time they went over a bump or around a corner. They went faster and faster, until suddenly, without warning, Mikey hit a tree root that was sticking out of the snow. He fell and rolled down the slope, turning into a big snowball with a little angel in the middle of it. *Wham!* He came to a sudden stop as the angel snowball hit a tree.

"Where am I? Who are you? What time is it?" Mikey said, shaking his head and spitting snow out of his mouth.

Gabe helped Mikey dig himself out of his snowball and find his skis, his hat, and his gloves. He wiped Mikey's nose, brushed him off, and sat him down on a rock. "Didn't you see that sign at the top of the run?"

"What sign?" asked Mikey sheepishly.

"There was a big yellow sign with red letters that said Hazards Exist That Are Not Marked," said Gabe.

"What's a hazard?" asked Mikey.

"A hazard is a danger. A hazard is something that could hurt you. When it's not marked, it means that there is no warning. That's why they put the sign there. If you had read the sign, maybe you would have been able to avoid the tree root, but maybe not. That's the point of today's lesson. You can't avoid all the hazards of life, because most of them are just not marked."

"I don't get it," said Mikey. "What good is it to tell people that there are things ahead that could hurt them when there's nothing they can do about it? That's not fair. The only way to avoid all the hazards is never to ski, right? If you decide to ski, you will probably hit some unmarked hazard sometime somewhere, and then *wham*, you get turned into an angel snowball."

"Exactly," said Gabe. "That's the truth about skiing. It's also the truth about life. If you are going to live a good and full life, and not just hide under your bed, there's always the chance that you'll get hurt along the way—"

"I get it," Mikey interrupted, "you have to be careful when you ski, but you can't expect to get down the mountain without ever falling. Sometimes you fall because you are just a klutz, but sometimes you fall because you hit an unmarked hazard."

"Right," said Gabe proudly. "And when you do fall, what should you do?"

"Just pick yourself up, wipe yourself off, and keep on going, because there's a whole lot more mountain to see before you reach the bottom."

"I'm so proud of you," said Gabe. "And remember that what is true about our skiing today is true about life every day. Life, like the ride down the mountain, is so beautiful and so much fun that it is worth taking the ride. Of course, you must be careful. There are many hazards you can avoid if you just don't live too fast or ski too fast, but you must also be brave because—"

"I know," said Mikey. "Because hazards exist that are not marked!"

Gabe laughed and said, "Yes. And just one more

thing to remember: It's not just haza[rds] not marked in skiing and in life. Blessings [and] beautiful things aren't always marked, either."

"Huh?" said Mikey, puzzled. "What do you mean?"

"I mean that great things also exist that are not marked, like when you find a beautiful shell on the beach, or a new friend in a place you were not sure you wanted to go to, or a sunset that was perfect at just the time you looked. It's what makes the journey down the mountain, and the journey through life, so wonderful, even if you fall now and then."

"How about one more run down the mountain?" Mikey pleaded.

And so the two angels flew back to the top of the mountain and shooshed their way down, giving themselves to the laws of gravity and chance. Their course was like a big hug of the mountain. Each turn of their skis churned up powdery, deep snow that flew into the air and returned to the mountain in a shower of a million frozen rainbows.

## Things to think about . . .

*You can't go through life without getting hurt. It's sad but true, because hazards exist that are not*

...ght be going too fast, or ...ing careful, and you could ...you might even make good ...rt anyway. There is just no way ...getting hurt sometimes. But here is ...hing. Even though there will be times ...ou get hurt and you don't expect it, there ...also be times when you are loved and don't expect it. There will be times when you meet a person who turns out to be your best friend or maybe even your wife or your husband, and you didn't expect it at all.

The whole idea is to just keep skiing down the mountain. Just keep living and loving and doing good things, and don't worry. Life is a great adventure—mostly fun and only sometimes bumpy. Anyway, even the hurts and bumps of life are important because they make you stronger and braver and more careful and more loving. Complaining about how unfair life is whenever you hit an unmarked hazard doesn't get you any-where. See what happens when you don't complain and just get going again. Chances are you'll find that a whole bunch of skiers will be following _you_ down the mountain.

Hopefully your life won't be filled with too many unmarked hazards, but just remember, life is also filled with a zillion of those unmarked blessings. God gives those to us. It's our job to find them.

# 3

## The Glowers:

### *Where is God in the bad times?*

"There's something I need to show you," Gabe said to Mikey.

Gabe and Mikey were sitting on a cloud watching the sun set and night take over from day. The sky was red and orange and purple and yellow and blue all at the same time, and it was changing every minute. When the daylight finally got lost over the edge of the world, Gabe said to Mikey,

"Heaven is beautiful, but there is almost nothing in Heaven as beautiful as this."

"Yeah," said Mikey. "I love sunsets."

"Look down there, Mikey, and tell me what you see," said Gabe.

Mikey was confused. "I see nothing except for some lights down there."

"What kinds of lights do you see?" Gabe asked.

"Nothing special. I see streetlights and car headlights, and the lights from a new burger place just opening up, and . . . I see some other lights, but I don't know what they are, exactly."

"Look harder, Mikey. Look at the lights that have nothing to do with cars or burgers. Look at those lights again," Gabe said.

"Gabe, if there is something you want me to see, you'd better show it to me, because I'm not seeing it on my own."

Gabe laughed and said, "Follow me down there." When they were close to the ground, Gabe said to Mikey, "Follow the brightest lights, little angel, follow the brightest lights."

Mikey squinted his eyes and said, "Yeah, the brightest lights are coming from that building over there. It must be one of those car stores or maybe the opening of a new restaurant. No, wait, it's not that . . . it's . . . I can't see without going closer."

"So go closer and you will see," Gabe said. They swooped down to the street, where Mikey finally saw where the bright lights were coming from: faces. People with glowing faces were serving food to poor people, who were hungry but had no money to buy food.

"They call it a soup kitchen, even though they serve more than soup," Gabe explained.

"Yikes!" screamed Mikey. "Who lit up those people?"

"God lit them up," said Gabe. "Well, really it's the good in them that lights them up. God made people so that the more good they do, the more they glow. When people do a little good in their lives, they glow a little, and when they do a lot of good, they glow a lot. We angels call good-deed-doing-people Glowers. The big Glowers shine so brightly that we can see them from Heaven."

"Wow!" said Mikey. "Can other people see the Glowers?"

"No. Only angels—and of course, God—can see people that glow."

"The color of the Glowers looks familiar to me," said Mikey.

"It should look familiar," said Gabe. "The color of the Glowers is the same color as the glow that comes from the place in Heaven that is closest to God."

"This is cool," said Mikey.

"It sure is," said Gabe.

After that night Mikey would gather with his friends to watch the sun set on earth and to count the Glowers. Even though Mikey learned how to spot Glowers during the day, it was always easier to see them at night. No light bulb or headlight had the same color as the Glowers.

Another time when Mikey really noticed Glowers was on the bright morning of September 11, 2001. He saw millions of angels flying over to one place. He flew with them and saw that Gabe was standing there with all the other angels. Mikey asked Gabe, "What's going on?"

Gabe was silent for a while and then said quietly, "A terrible thing just happened. We are getting ready to go and help. This is a big emergency. God is sending all the spare angels and even the guardian-angels-in-training down to earth to help."

Then a horn sounded in Heaven, and suddenly millions of angels were diving off clouds and flying to earth. On the way down Gabe explained to Mikey that some very angry people had just flown some big jet airplanes into the two tallest buildings in New York City and into a building in Washington, D.C. They were about to crash another plane somewhere else, but the people on that plane stopped them by crashing the plane into an empty field in Pennsylvania. "Many people were killed this morning," Gabe said. "It is very sad. It is very scary. We need to be down there to help all the people who are dying and hurt and scared."

"I'm scared, too," said Mikey. "Who is gonna help me?"

"God is going to help all of us, but it is going to take time, and it is going to be hard," said Gabe. They flew on in the flood of angels like little fish in a big school of fish swimming very fast together.

Finally Gabe and Mikey got to the place in New York City where the buildings had been hit by the planes but before the buildings crashed down. They flew right into the upper floors, just below where the planes hit. Smoke and fire were everywhere. People were screaming, "Help us! Help us!"

"Go help them, little angel. Go help them!" Gabe said as he flew off into the smoke and fire and dust. Mikey walked through a door and saw a Glower call his wife on his cell phone and say to her, "Honey, I love you. I will see you in Heaven." Then he hung up his phone and collapsed. Just then something bumped into Mikey from behind. It was Gabe. He was leading a firefighter who was carrying a man in a wheelchair down the stairs.

Mikey didn't know which way to turn. Just then he saw a dog. It was a guide dog leading a blind man. Both the dog and the man were coughing. They could not find their way out. Mikey led the dog and the man to the stairs. There they saw angels and Glowers and people coughing and crying and screaming. Mikey had never seen anything like it ever, ever, ever. They walked down stairs and stairs, crowded with people. After what seemed like a few hours, they got down to the ground and ran out into the street. The street was not much better, but the smoke and dust were not as bad. Gabe was down there already and screamed at Mikey, "Get them away from the buildings *now*!" They ran and ran and got to a place where some firefighters and police were helping people. They had made it out. Mikey then flew back into the building again and again, trying to help people get out.

Suddenly a huge roar and rumble shook the building, and it began to crash down. Mikey flew out a window and saw the building crash down. Angels were flying everywhere, but through the dust Mikey could see the Glowers helping people on the street. And then Mikey saw a tower of sparks flying up from the ground, through the dust and smoke and into the air, straight up, higher and higher.

"God is taking them straight to Heaven," Gabe said, choking on his tears. "Those sparks are the souls of all the people who died here today. God is taking them straight up to Heaven. Almost always when a person dies, the angel who watched over that person takes his or her soul to Heaven. But today, Mikey, it is God who is taking them all up to Heaven."

"I will never understand this," Mikey said softly.

"Nobody understands this," Gabe said. "Let's go home now."

As they flew back to Heaven, all the angels were part of the tower of sparks reaching to Heaven. The sparks from the fire were rising into the sky like a huge tornado of little lights. On the way back to Heaven, a gentle rain washed off all the dust and dirt from the angels who had flown down to earth to help. To most of the angels it just looked like rain, but Gabe hugged Mikey and whispered to him, "These are God's tears."

## Things to think about . . .

*Not only is God with us in the bad times, God is especially with us in the bad times. Those are the times when we are scared and need hope and love, and those are what God brings us. God also sends us helpers in the bad times. Maybe it's someone in your family, maybe it's a friend, or maybe it's* someone you don't even know. And who knows, maybe God sends us angels like Gabe and Mikey who are God's helpers.

The attack on America on September 11 was a tragic time. It was a scary time, but it was not a time without God. Even then, God reminded us that there is way more love in the world than hate. On September 11, we all saw the worst things that people can do, but we also saw the best things that people can do. Those good people remind us that even if the bad people in the world win today, they will not win tomorrow. On our darkest days, God is not farthest away from us, but right near us, giving us courage and hope. One thing I believe for sure: God was with each and every person in those towers that day.

In this story, Gabe taught Mikey about Glowers. In real life, of course, people don't glow—at least not with light we can see. That's just a way to imagine what it might look like to God. But the truth is, what you do in your life shows up somehow. And for sure, God can see it from miles away.

# 4

## Pretend Dancing:

*What can I do when I'm supposed
to feel happy but I don't?*

After September 11, Mikey realized what it felt like to be truly sad. Up until that point, Mikey had never known real sadness. Life in Heaven was pretty nice. He was happy most of the time until then.

He wasn't the only sad angel in Heaven.

The scene that day in New York City and Washington, D.C., and in that field in Pennsylvania was very bad. The scene in Heaven was sad and confusing, too. So many souls came up to Heaven that day after they died. Most of them were people who never expected to die so young. "Where am I? What happened? Why did this happen to me?" The angels didn't know what to say, and everybody was crying. Mikey just flew around trying to help out in any way he could. After a while, he felt so sad that all he wanted to do was hide in a cloud, which is exactly what he did . . . for a long time. He needed to be alone.

After a few weeks, things in Heaven were still pretty sad. Angels were just moping around. Mikey was not hiding in a cloud anymore, but he was still not a happy angel.

One morning Gabe said to Mikey, "Hey, how about going over to the musicians' cloud and listening to some music? Maybe music will cheer you up."

"Nothing will cheer me up. I'm still too sad."

Gabe grabbed Mikey's hand and pulled him along.

"I want to be left alone, Gabe."

But in a whoosh they were on the musicians' cloud. It was a big cloud because lots of angels always came over to hear their favorite music.

"I want to get out of here. I don't feel like listening to music."

"Come on. Just stay for one song," Gabe said to Mikey.

"Okay, one song and I'm gone." Mikey sat down.

Gabe nodded to the band, and they started to play an old rock-and-roll song called "Twist and Shout." Mikey looked up. "That's my favorite song!"

"I know," said Gabe as the music got louder. Soon all the angels there got up and started dancing. They were waving their arms and flapping their wings, and some of them were even dancing upside down!

"Let's dance, too," Gabe screamed over the loud music.

"I don't feel like dancing," said Mikey.

"Okay, then just pretend dance," said Gabe.

"What is pretend dancing?" asked Mikey, his head still in his hands.

"Pretend dancing is when you don't really feel like dancing but you dance anyway. Come on, just do one pretend dance and then we'll go."

"Well, okay," said Mikey as he got up and joined Gabe and the other angels.

At first, Mikey was just moving from side to side. He wasn't moving his arms or his feet or his wings. He was just sort of . . . pretend dancing. But after a while, his feet started to move and his wings started to flap, and finally he was waving his arms and singing with the music. Mikey was smiling and singing, and by the end of the song he was even dancing upside down. When the song ended, he clapped and whistled and shouted, "Yeah! All right! Wow!"

On the way home Mikey said, "Thanks, Gabe. I thought there was only one kind of dancing. Teaching me about pretend dancing was one of the best things you've ever taught me. The only way to go from not dancing at all to real dancing is to pretend dance for a little while. I *wanted* to hide out in my cloud, but I *needed* to get going again."

Mikey danced back home, and several times

during the days that followed, even when he wasn't dancing with his feet, he was dancing inside.

## Things to think about . . .

*What Mikey learned about pretend dancing is something that we all need to learn. Some days we are happy and don't need help. Some days we go through life with no problems at all. Those are the days when real dancing is easy. But on other days, on the days when we are sad or lonely or broken or afraid, it's very hard to do even normal, everyday things. On those days, we want to hide under the covers and be left alone. That's okay for a while, but then we have to get up and get on with our lives. We have to go to school and do our homework and help out at home.*

*The best way to get back to our normal lives is to learn how to pretend dance like Gabe taught Mikey. If we just get up and do the things we have to do, even if our hearts aren't really in them, that's okay. Maybe later in the day, or maybe tomorrow or maybe the day after tomorrow, or maybe in a few days or maybe in a few weeks, we* will find that we are not pretend dancing anymore. We will find that we are real dancing. We *will* smile and laugh again. When things are bad, it may seem like we'll never smile or laugh again . . . but we will.

There's just one more thing. When you go from pretend dancing to real dancing, do not try to dance upside down!

# 5

## People Are Not Nickels:

### Does God love some people more than others?

"I have an assignment for you," said Gabe.

"Oh, Gabe, can't it wait? Raziel, Wilhelmina, and I were just about to play a really awesome game," said Mikey.

"Nope. Sorry. It can't wait. Your friends can join you in the assignment. I need each of you to find me the person that God loves the most," said Gabe. "And if you can show me the person that

God loves the most, you will get an A in this class . . . and a nickel."

Mikey scratched his head. "I understand giving the winner an A, but what's the nickel for?"

"You'll find out soon enough," said Gabe. "Now get out of here and don't forget to take your cameras with you so that you can fly down to earth and take a picture of the person you think God loves the most."

Mikey and his friends grabbed their cameras and dove down to earth.

The next day the three angels were buzzing with excitement.

"I'm winning this contest for sure!" said Raziel, holding his picture close to his chest so that nobody could see it.

"No way," said Wilhelmina. "I have right here a picture of the person God loves the most."

Mikey didn't say a word.

"Calm down now, let's just calm down," said Gabe. "Okay, who wants to begin?"

"I do! I do!" said Wilhelmina. She pulled out a picture of a woman in a white coat looking into the ear of a little girl with some kind of ear flashlight.

"She's a kid doctor. They call them pediatricians. Her name is Dr. Esmeralda Fendergender, and I am sure that God loves doctors more than anybody else. We all know that God wants people to be healed from all the bad stuff they get. Doctors do that. Doctors heal people, so doctors are doing God's work. It's very clear, God loves doctors more than anybody."

"Very nice, Wilhelmina," said Gabe with a smile. "Thank you. Does anyone else have another choice for who God loves most?"

"I do," said Raziel. He proudly showed Gabe a picture of a newborn baby. "This is Ezekiel. I picked Ezekiel because he was just being born when I got to earth, and I believe that God loves babies most of all. Babies are so little and helpless. Babies remind God that *all people* are really pretty little and pretty helpless, and they need God's help and one another's help. I also think that God loves babies most because babies have not made any bad choices yet. They are the only pure people. As people get older, they make more and more choices, and some of those choices are bad. Babies are just little and good, and that's why

I thought God must surely love them the most and the best."

"Fine work, Raziel," said Gabe. "Fine work indeed. Is there anybody else?"

Gabe flew over to Mikey and asked him to show him the picture of his choice. "Oh, it's nobody special," Mikey said quietly.

Mikey showed Gabe a picture of an old woman pushing a shopping cart filled with old bottles and cans she had picked out of the garbage. "I don't even know her name," said Mikey.

"Then why did you pick her?" Gabe asked.

"I picked her," Mikey said, "because she was the very first person I saw when I whooshed down to earth to begin this assignment."

"You picked the first person you saw as the person God loves the most?" asked Gabe.

"Yup," said Mikey. "I picked her to show that God loves all people exactly the same . . . nobody more than anybody else, and nobody less than anybody else. I picked the first person I saw because any person would have been just as good in the eyes of God."

Gabe didn't say a word. He just wrapped up

Mikey in his arms and in his big wings and hugged him and said to him softly, "God bless you, my little angel. God bless you. I thought I was your teacher, but today you were mine."

Gabe gave Mikey an A. And then he reached into his pocket and gave Mikey a nickel.

"Gabe, why the nickel?" asked Mikey, grinning broadly.

Gabe answered, "When the U.S. Mint makes nickels for the people who use American money, every nickel has the picture of Thomas Jefferson on it. Every nickel looks exactly the same, and every nickel is worth exactly the same. When God makes people in the image of God, God's picture is also on every person. *But* every person looks different. Even so, every person is worth exactly the same because every person is made in the image of God. By picking the first person you saw, Mikey, you showed me that you knew this. No matter who you are guarding, you must never forget that every person is loved by God and is just as special to God as every other person in the world. That's how people are different from nickels."

**Things to think about . . .**

*It's hard to remember that God loves every person the same. Maybe you should keep a nickel in your pocket to remember that. When you see somebody who is making good choices, God loves that person just as much as the person you see making bad choices. God loves tall people the same as short people, fat people the same as thin people, beautiful people the same as ugly people. We are all worth the same to God.*

*Maybe the thing God wants most is for us to love one another the way God loves us. Maybe that's the most important thing we can do. So if you are loved—by your family, by your friends, by your pets, by God—then take some of that love you have been blessed with and spread that love around to people who may not have not been loved as much as you. You just might find out that when you give something away, you truly find it.*

# 6

# Sticks in a Bundle Are Unbreakable:

### How can I help others who are hurting?

"We're going camping?" asked Mikey, looking at Gabe.

"That's right," said Gabe. "Camping is the only way to learn today's lesson about life."

Suddenly they were in a beautiful forest with a clear, wide river running through it. The river gurgled its way through the forest almost as if it was singing a song to the world.

"This is a very beautiful place, Gabe. How did you find it?" asked Mikey.

"Oh, the world is full of beautiful places," said Gabe. "I come here a lot to rest and think and clear my mind. Let's set up our tents right here." So Gabe and Mikey set up their tents near the riverbank. Then Gabe said, "Now let's make a campfire. Gather some little sticks for the kindling and some branches and logs for the fire."

"Are you sure angels need to know how to make a campfire?"

"Definitely," said Gabe.

"Okay, okay," said Mikey as he scurried off into the woods, soon returning with a big pile of sticks and branches. He stacked the wood between his wings, which impressed even Gabe.

"You are a regular outdoor angel, Mikey," said Gabe. "Good work. Now break one stick and put it in the middle of our fire pit."

Mikey snapped one of the sticks in half using just one hand. "That was easy," he said.

"Now take five sticks, hold them together in a

bundle, and break them up for kindling wood for our fire."

Mikey held five sticks together and tried to break them, but he couldn't do it. He huffed and he puffed, and he twisted and he grunted, and he made all sorts of noises and then, finally, gave up. "I can't break them when they are in a bundle. I can only break them one at a time."

"Right!" said Gabe, "That's the first part of today's lesson. Now it's time to get going."

"Whoa there, boss. We just spent all this time pitching camp and making the fire, and now you want to leave right away. Let's stay and enjoy this place awhile; it's pretty and I need the rest."

"Nope," said Gabe. "We have to finish the lesson."

Gabe and Mikey were suddenly in a house that was filled with people who were just finishing reading and singing some prayers. After the prayers were over, some people sat and talked quietly, while others had coffee and cake in the kitchen. Upstairs the two angels saw a group of girls who were gathered around one girl who was crying.

"What's going on here?" asked Mikey.

"This is the Goldman house. Sara Goldman's father just died. These people are Jewish, and this gathering at their house is called a *shiva*. Shiva is the week after a Jewish person dies, when people come over to the house to sit with the family and comfort them. Those are Sara's friends around her, and downstairs her mother's friends are gathered around her."

"That sounds nice," said Mikey.

"Yes, it sure is, and actually every religion has something like shiva. The idea that people should come and comfort people who have just lost a loved one is a very good and very old idea. Catholics call their comforting time a wake. Come on, Mikey, I want to visit another house of mourning not far from here."

In the blink of an eye, Gabe and Mikey were in another house, but it was mostly dark. Upstairs they found a girl who was about ten or eleven years old. She was crying on her bed.

"Who is she?" asked Mikey.

"Her name is Jasmine, and her father also just died. The funeral was today," answered Gabe.

"Where are the people? Where are her friends?"

"Jasmine has friends, but she didn't call them because she thought she wanted to be alone. They didn't call her because they thought she wanted to be alone.

"Time to go, Mikey. Today's lesson is over now."

"Wait! I want to help Jasmine feel better. I'm worried about her. Let me stay, please let me stay."

"You can't fix what's wrong here, Mikey. You can't fix this."

Mikey was very quiet on the way back to Heaven. Gabe hugged Mikey and kissed him good night and flew off. Suddenly Mikey screamed, *"I understand the sticks! I understand the sticks!"* He flew like a rocket and caught up with Gabe. "I get it; I understand the lesson of the sticks."

"Tell me, my little angel. Tell me what you learned."

"I learned," Mikey said proudly, "that sticks in a bundle are unbreakable, but sticks alone can be broken by anybody. Jasmine was just one stick. She was all alone in her sadness, and that made her very breakable and extra sad. Sara was like a stick in a bundle. She was also very sad, but she was made stronger because her friends were around her when she was most breakable. When people are sad, they need to be bundled up with other people and not be alone when they are suffering. Is that the lesson of the sticks, Gabe? Is that the lesson?"

"Congratulations, Mikey," said Gabe. "You figured it out."

And together they said an angel prayer, thanking God for making such a beautiful world. They watched the sun set over the clear, wide river that gurgled its way through the forest almost as if it was singing a song to the world.

### Things to think about . . .

*There is a big difference between breaking your leg and breaking your heart. When you break your leg, a doctor puts it in a cast, and then you wait around for a few months and <u>presto</u>, your leg is healed all by itself. But when you have a broken heart, when something happens to you that makes you so sad that you feel like you are crying inside, your heart cannot heal all by itself. You need friends and family around you to heal from sad-*

*ness. When you are sad and alone, you are like one single stick, but when you are sad and with people who love you, you are like a bundled stick. That's what Mikey learned by visiting Jasmine and Sara. Jasmine was alone and Sara was bundled. Being bundled does not mean that you never break; it just means that when you do break, you heal up much faster because you have people around you who love you, who will hug you and hold you and wait for your broken heart to become whole again.*

*Your friends and your family are good bundlers. God is a great bundler, too. When you are sad and you pray to God, God will come to you and hold you and comfort you. The way God comes to you is not the same way people come to you. You can't see God, but you can feel God. The feeling of being loved and protected by God is the same kind of feeling you have when you are loved and protected by anyone who cares for you. It's a great feeling to know that God is always ready to bundle you.*

*The clergy who work at the place where you go to pray—your church or your synagogue or your mosque or your temple—are also good bundlers. They do God's work, which is a good thing.*

*Sometimes a psychologist or psychiatrist or coun-selor or teacher at your school can be a good bundler. All these people, and God, can help you feel that you are not going through the bad stuff in your life all alone. That feeling is so important in healing a broken heart.*

*You can also be a good bundler to your friends. When you call up a sad friend, or see that person at school, you could say something like, "I heard you were sad, and I'm sorry. Is there anything I can do for you?" By saying that, you are being a great bundler by showing that you care. You can't keep that person from feeling sad, but you can keep that person from feeling alone. When you take time to bundle others, you will be surprised at how many people will bundle you when you are sad. Some days you are the bundler, and some days you are the bundlee. That's not only the way sticks work. It's the way life works.*

# 7

## Spot Died Today:

### Is it okay if I'm really mad at God?

"I've got something I want you to read," Gabe said to Mikey as he handed him a letter. "It's from Jennifer. Read it out loud to me. I want to know what you think we should do about it."

So Mikey began:

*Dear God,*
*I'm so mad at you! Today you let my dog Spot die. Spot was a good dog with a*

black wet nose. Sometimes when I came home from school, his tail would wag so hard that he'd knock things over. He was old and could not jump up on my bed anymore, but I helped him get up and he slept right next to my feet. If I ever had a bad dream, I would wake up and touch Spot with my feet, and then I would feel better. Spot and I grew up together, and I loved him with all my heart since he was a puppy and I was a baby.

He was only ten years old when he died. People say that's like seventy years old in dog years, which doesn't make any sense to me. I don't see why dogs don't have the same years as people. Anyway, he got cancer and died, and I'm mad at you, God, because you took Spot away from me. I will never understand why you did that, and I will never forgive you.

I hope you have other people who still believe in you, because I'm not sure how I feel about you, God.

Jennifer

"She is very angry," Mikey said. "I don't think we could tell her anything that would make her less angry at God. She loved her dog. Her dog died. And she blames God. I don't know what to do for her."

"You are right, Mikey," said Gabe. "Jennifer is so angry, she won't listen to anything we tell her. I have an idea, though, that will show you another way we angels can help people without pushing them or telling them. We call it d-mail."

"D-mail? What's d-mail?"

"A d-mail is a dream message that we can send to any person on earth. Many people think that dreams are just wild stuff they think up that doesn't mean anything. That is true about some dreams. But other dreams are messages from angels. God even sends a few of them."

"How does a d-mail work?"

"Well, we think it up and write it down and then send the dream over. You see, in a dream we can show people things that we can't show them when they are awake because either they would not listen or it would freak them out."

"Yeah, but don't most people forget their dreams?" asked Mikey.

"Yes, they do. But the big dreams with big messages stay with most people a long time. So why don't you think about Jennifer's problem and write out a d-mail for her, and we will send it down so that she isn't so angry at God."

"Cool!" said Mikey, who flew off to write a dream for Jennifer. He returned later that afternoon with some papers filled with writing.

Gabe read the dream. "This is great, Mikey. Good work. I hope it helps Jennifer."

That night Jennifer crawled into her bed. She did not say her prayers because she was so angry at God. She moved her feet around under the blanket, trying to touch Spot. Then she cried herself to sleep.

Next Jennifer felt something at her feet. She sat up in bed and looked down and saw Spot sleeping there. "Spot, you're alive!" she screamed. She hugged him and heard his tail thumping on the bed.

Suddenly two more dogs jumped up on Jennifer's bed, and she screamed, "Yikes! Who are you?" One was a gray dog with blue eyes, and the other was a yellow dog with sad eyes and a wet black nose like Spot's. Before Jennifer could reach down to pet them, five more dogs jumped up on her bed. She could hardly move and didn't know what to do. She screamed for her mom and dad, but they couldn't hear her. Jennifer finally got out from under her covers and squirmed out of her bed, which was now totally filled with dogs. She put her feet down on the rug, but the rug was furry, and it moved and barked when she touched it. It was morning, and Jennifer could see that her floor was filled with dogs. There must have been a hundred dogs in her bedroom.

"Excuse me, excuse me!" Jennifer said as she tried to walk over and around the dogs. She opened the door to her room, after clearing out a few dogs, and saw that the hallway was full of dogs. The bathroom was full of dogs. There were even dogs sleeping in the sink and bathtub.

"Daddy! Mommy!" she screamed. "Help me!" But nobody answered her.

Jennifer made her way down the hall, and with each step she heard, "Woof! Yowl! Woof!" as she stepped on a carpet of dogs. She tumbled downstairs and crawled over a pile of dogs and ran outside and saw that her lawn was full of dogs so that she couldn't see the grass. There were dogs in the garden and dogs down the path, dogs down the street and dogs in the trees. High up in the branches of the big maple tree in her backyard, Jennifer saw her mom and dad. They were out on a branch hanging on.

They waved at her and said, "Hi, Jennifer. How are you, honey?"

"How am I?" she screamed. "There are dogs everywhere! What happened? What's going on here?"

"Oh, don't you remember, dear?" they said. "You wanted Spot to never die, so God granted your wish. Spot will never die. He will be with us forever, but so will all the other dogs of all the other kids who loved them, too. No dogs die anymore. And because new puppies are being born, but no old dogs die, the world just got filled up with dogs. This branch is the only place left, but if you climb up here we can squeeze over and make room for you."

Jennifer looked at the millions of dogs and screamed, "Nooooooooooooooooooooooooooooooo!" And then she woke up from her dream.

The next morning at breakfast Jennifer looked at her mom and dad and said, "It's okay that Spot died. I am still sad and I miss him very much, but I am not angry at God anymore. I understand now that if no old dogs died, there would be no room for new dogs to be born. Death is sad, but death is a part of life. I am okay now."

Her parents got up from the table and came over to Jennifer and gave her big hugs and kisses, and some of their tears dripped onto her pancakes.

Her dad said, "We are so proud of you, honey. You're very brave and very wise for such a little girl. And honey, would you mind going to the pantry to get me some more maple syrup for my pancakes? It's on the bottom shelf."

Jennifer walked over to the pantry. There was a cardboard box filled with torn-up newspapers— and a little puppy with a black nose and a wagging tail that thumped against the side of the box.

"Oh, God! Thank you! Thank you! He's so cute. Oh Mommy, Daddy, I love you so much. Thank you!" Jennifer picked up the puppy and held him and laughed as he licked her face.

"What do you want to call him?" Jennifer's mom asked her.

Jennifer thought and said, "I want to call him Mikey."

Gabe looked at Mikey and said, "Woof!" Then Gabe gave him a hug and whooshed him back to Heaven to make sure Spot was comfortable forever in his new home.

**Things to think about . . .**

*Of course, d-mail is just a fun idea about how dreams come to us. We don't know who "writes" our dreams, but I believe that God uses dreams to speak to us—if we're listening.*

*Sometimes when we're really mad at God, it's because we don't understand. But if we understood everything, we'd be God.*

*Sometimes people are angry at God because some person or animal they really loved has died. Sometimes they are angry at God because life just seems unfair. Sometimes people keep their anger at God inside them for a long time. This doesn't hurt*

God, but it can hurt other people because anger eats up the good parts inside you. Anger makes you bitter and sour and grumpy and no fun to be around.

But remember, it's okay with God if you're angry with God. One way to let go of that anger is to learn what Jennifer learned . . . that we don't know all the answers, only God does. Jennifer learned that death is a part of life. If nothing died, there would soon be no room here on earth for babies and puppies. Every baby and every puppy (and kitten and hamster) is taking the place of some- body or some animal who died. That's why some parents name babies after people they love who have died. It is a way of remembering an old life and celebrating a new life at the same time.

Anyway, it's okay to be angry at God, because your anger is just a sign that you care. For Jennifer, it was a sign that she loved her dog and was very sad to see him die. God would rather have you be angry at God than not speak to God at all. And you'll see, chances are that speaking to God will help you lose the anger and keep the love.

# 8

## Going Up:

### What happens to us after we die?

"Come on, Mikey, hurry! Fred doesn't have much time left before he goes up," Gabe said to Mikey as he shook him from a deep sleep.

"Who? What? Where? Who's Fred? Where is he going up? Where are we going? What time is it? Gabe, where are we going? I need my sleep."

Gabe yanked Mikey out of his cloud and whooshed him down to earth. The two of them stood near an old man in a hospital bed. There were people standing around the bed looking at him.

Some of them were crying softly. One of them, an older woman who looked like Fred's wife, was holding his hand and speaking to him. He didn't seem to hear her. "Fred, my darling. Everyone is here. The children are here and your grandchildren are outside in the waiting room. They gave me pictures they painted for you. Honey, we all know how hard you fought to live, but the doctors tell us that there is nothing else they can do for you. It's okay to let go now, my love. It's okay to let go. I just want you to know that I love you with all my heart."

"Me too, Daddy!" said a woman who was holding a painted picture of a flower and crying loudly.

"Me too. I love you, Fred," said the husband of the crying woman.

"Me too, me too. We love you, Dad. We love you." Each person around the bed spoke and kissed Fred on the forehead and then turned away and cried.

"Honey," the older woman said, "a part of you is going up now, but a part of you will stay down here with us forever." Then she laid her head on Fred's chest and cried a cry Mikey had never heard before. It was a low cry that shook her like a leaf in a big wind.

Gabe moved forward and touched Fred, and then something came out of Fred that floated above him in the room. It was gray and you could kind of see through it, but not really. It looked like Fred when he was younger and really healthy.

"What is that?" Mikey hardly had the breath to ask Gabe.

"That's Fred's soul," Gabe answered softly. "Fred just died. I wanted you to see how this happens. I wanted you to see how souls go up."

"Can they see his soul?" asked Mikey, pointing at all the people in the room.

"No. They can't see his soul. They can't see us."

"But I can see you!" said Fred as he floated over and stood next to Mikey and Gabe. "Who are you? Where am I? What's happening?" asked Fred's soul.

"Hello, Fred. My name is Gabriel. I have been your guardian angel for your whole life. I have

**54**

watched over you for God and tried to help and protect you. I am sorry you died, but it's good to talk to you finally and to tell you that I thought you lived a great life and that you were a terrific person."

"Thank you, Gabriel. Who is that?" Fred asked, looking at Mikey.

"I'm sorry, Fred," Gabe apologized. "This is Michael, my student. Someday soon he is going to be a guardian angel."

"Nice to meet you," said Mikey. "They call me Mikey in Heaven, and they call him Gabe."

"Fred, Mikey and I are here to take you up."

"Up to where?" asked Fred's soul.

"Up to Heaven," answered Gabe.

The machine near the bed beeped a long beep, doctors rushed in, and everyone cried. They covered Fred's body with a sheet and took it away.

Fred's family hugged one another. After a while they went home to make plans for Fred's funeral. Gabe took Fred's hand, and they flew right through the ceiling in the hospital room and right through the roof, and right into the night sky and right up, higher and higher.

On the way Mikey asked Fred, "What was it like to die?"

Fred answered, "It felt like I was getting out of bed in the morning, except that I was getting out of my body instead of a bed. Boy, was I surprised to see you guys! I really didn't believe in souls or angels or Heaven or anything when I was alive. I sort of believed in God, but to tell you the truth I wasn't even sure about God. I just can't believe it; everything I didn't believe in turns out to be real!"

"Lots of souls are surprised," Gabe said. "This is a very big change for you. I understand. Don't worry about anything. You are safe, and you are going to Heaven now."

"Yeah," said Mikey to Fred's soul, "Heaven is really cool. You are going to love the place."

They reached the gates of Heaven and flew to a sign that read All New Souls Check In Here. A bunch of angels were working there, and each soul standing in line had a guardian angel holding his or her hand. The angel behind the desk said, "Welcome to Heaven, Fred. Please go over there and get fitted for your robe, halo, and wings."

Gabe took Fred over to the place where the sign read Robes Here. Get Your Robes Here. The fitting angel looked at Fred's soul and asked, "Do you want zippers?"

"Yeah, get zippers!" said Mikey.

"Why do I need zippers?" asked Fred's soul.

"If you fly upside down or loop the loop, the zippers keep the stuff from falling out of your pockets," said Mikey in a low voice that he thought Gabe could not hear.

"No zippers," said Gabe, frowning at Mikey.

After Fred's soul got a clean, new, white robe, they took him past the sign with a red arrow pointing straight ahead that read Halo House This Way.

When they got there, the angel clerk said, "Hello, sir, let me just fit you for a halo." The angel fiddled around in a box of halos that sparked and lit up and fizzled. Finally he found one and put it over Fred's head and smiled. "It's just right for you. Now here is your halo sock."

"My halo sock?" Fred's soul asked with a puzzled look.

"Don't ever lose your halo sock," Mikey said in

a stern voice. "Those halos are so bright, they light up a whole cloud, and nobody can sleep at night unless we cover them up. So every night before we go to sleep, all of us angels cover our halos with halo socks. You can decide later how to decorate your halo sock. Just don't lose it, or you will be sleeping at the very edge of Heaven every night."

Then they took Fred's soul to the place where there were thousands of sets of wings on hooks. An angel looked Fred over and said, "No question about it. You need size nine wings."

Fred got his wings attached, and then Mikey showed him how to fly a little. "You see, flying with wings is sort of like moving your shoulders and arms back and forth like a chicken. It's hard to explain, but it's not that hard to do."

"Just be careful," the wing fitter angel added. "It takes a while to figure out how to use wings. Whatever you do, don't try flying upside down or loop the loops while you are still learning."

Then Gabe and Mikey took Fred's soul over to a cloud where other souls were waiting and crying and cheering. Fred saw them and screamed,

"Momma! Momma!" He flew to her in a kind of wobbly way and she hugged him, and then all the other souls gathered around him and hugged and kissed him.

"What's going on?" Mikey asked Gabe.

"Those are the souls of Fred's family who already died and came up to Heaven. That is his mother, and over there is his father. There are also other relatives that Fred never even met and never even knew about. This is my favorite part of bringing souls to Heaven, Mikey. I just love to see souls meet up with the souls of the people they loved who died before them. I love to see souls learn where they got the shape of their nose or the color of their hair or their love of music. It is a very wonderful thing for souls to learn that they will now be together forever."

"Gabe, I'm sad that Fred died, but I'm happy that he got to see his mom again. Is that what you meant when you told me that God makes happy and sad fit together?"

"That's exactly what I meant," replied Gabe. "That's how God runs the world. Let's get going, Mikey. We should leave Fred alone with them now."

"Good luck, Fred," yelled Gabe.

Fred held up his hand and waved and said, "Thank you! Thank you, Gabe, for being my guardian angel. Mikey, it was nice to meet you, too. Good luck!" Mikey flew over and gave Fred a kiss and a hug and whispered something in his ear.

"What did you tell him?" Gabe asked Mikey as they flew off.

"Oh, nothing," said Mikey. "I just told him that he could always get zippers later."

## Things to think about . . .

*Nobody knows for sure what Heaven is really like. I think it would be neat if it was a place to get robes (with or without zippers), wings, and halos (with or without socks). I hope Heaven is like that, or even something like that, but whatever Heaven is like, I believe Heaven is real.*

*I believe that after we die, our souls get to see all the souls of all the people we loved a lot but who died while we were still alive. I believe this because I think that love is the connector between us and the people we loved who have died. Their love stays with us after they die and connects us to them. I* also believe that our love stays with them as they go up to Heaven, keeping them connected to us. Love is the great connector of everything good in the universe.

I think love also connects God to us. God's love helps us get through the sad times in our lives. We know that we are not alone and that God is taking care of the people we loved who die. I can't prove this, but I _know_ this. That is what I mean by faith. Faith is what you _know_ but can't prove. I know everything will be okay because I have faith that God loves us and will protect us. Maybe God uses angels like Mikey and Gabe, or maybe God uses some other way. However it works, I know it does work.

I can't explain souls, either, but I know souls are real. I believe that when our bodies die, something in us lives on. That something is our soul.

You can kind of see people's souls when they are laughing or smiling. Their faces light up. That light comes from the soul, and the soul comes from God. The soul is like the piece of God that is put in you when you are born and is taken out of you and brought back to God when you die.

Some people believe that souls get cleaned off and recycled and used again. Some people believe that the soul God put in you will never be put into any other person ever. Which do you believe is true? There are days when I think I was a bug once, but those are not my best days.

# 9

## It Mattered to That One:

### *Why even try when nothing I do makes any difference?*

"Today we're going to the beach," Gabe said to Mikey one bright and sunny day in Heaven.

"I love the beach—sitting in the sand, swimming in the water, building sand castles, or just listening to the waves," Mikey said.

"Let's go," said Gabe. The beach was full of people. "Look over there at that old man," said Gabe, pointing to an old man with a straw hat and skin that was tan and wrinkled from many days on the beach. The old man bent down, picked something up, and threw it into the ocean. He then moved on down the beach a few steps and did the same thing again.

"What's he doing?" asked Mikey.

"Just watch and listen," answered Gabe.

From down the beach came a young man, running at the edge of the surf. He passed the old man and stopped, breathing heavily from his run. He asked the old man with the straw hat, "What are you doing?"

The old man answered, "There was a storm last night. Lots of these starfish were washed up onto the beach. If I don't throw them back, the sun will dry them out and they'll be dead by noon."

The young jogger laughed and said, "You are a fool, old man. Look! This beach is miles long. Why, there must be thousands of starfish stranded on it. Most of them are dead or dying already, and you can't get to them all. Listen to me, old man. What you're doing just doesn't matter."

The old man did not look up and did not stop. He just bent over and picked up another starfish

**64**

from the beach and threw it into the safety of the waves, saying gently, "It mattered to that one."

"Time to go," said Gabe.

"What? You brought me down here to sit in the sand and watch a guy throw starfish into the ocean?"

"Okay, let's go now. We are late for a birthday party," Gabe said as he shook sand out of his wings.

Mikey caught up with Gabe at a bakery on a nice street in a town called Lindenhurst. A man got out of a white van and entered the bake shop under the sign that read Black Forest Bake Shoppe.

"Hi, Walter," the man said. "Got anything for me today?"

"Sure do, Sam. You can take all my bread from yesterday and the rolls and, oh yes, you can take that birthday cake, too. The woman who ordered it never came to pick it up. It would be a shame to just throw it out. It's a good thing that you guys at the soup kitchen are around. I hate throwing out good food."

"It's a good thing you're around too, Walter.

We're grateful for your bread and rolls. I guess we're a good team." Sam packed up the bread and rolls, and he put the cake in its box on the front seat next to him so it wouldn't get squashed. Sam drove off to another part of town with the two angels flying right behind. Soon he came to a store called The Mary Brennan Inn. People were lined up outside the store, quietly waiting for it to open.

"This is the place where I saw the Glowers! This is that soup kitchen where they serve more than soup to people who are hungry," Mikey said excitedly.

"That's right," answered Gabe, "but today I didn't bring you here to see the Glowers. I brought you here to see her." And Gabe pointed to a little girl standing in line holding on to her mother's hand. "Her name is Maria."

Sam unloaded Walter's bread and rolls and put them in a big bowl. Then he took out the beautifully decorated birthday cake and put it down at the end of the serving table along with the chicken, the green beans, and the mashed potatoes. Maria watched Sam with eyes as big as saucers. Then she let go of her mother's hand and ran down the line. She ran past the bread and the rolls, past the chicken with goopy gravy, past the mashed potatoes and the green beans. Maria ran right over to the birthday cake.

Maria read the icing on the cake, looked up at Sam with tears in her eyes, and asked, "How did you know it was my birthday?"

Maria's mother came up to them, and she was also crying. She said, "Maria is seven years old today, and she never ever had a birthday party or a birthday present or a birthday cake before. Thank you. Thank you so much."

Sam was crying now, but he dried his tears and said, "Hey, everybody, it's Maria's birthday!" And all the people in the soup kitchen that day sang "Happy Birthday" to Maria. She was smiling and laughing, and she got the first big piece of the cake.

Then an amazing thing happened. One homeless woman brought Maria her very best and only scarf. An old man sang Maria a blues song he had heard as a kid. People with nothing at all each gave Maria some kind of birthday present. After a time Maria and her mother left the soup kitchen with her presents, and of course, with the rest of the birthday cake.

The next time Sam visited Walter at his bakery to collect bread and rolls for the soup kitchen, he told Walter the story of Maria and her birthday cake. He said, "Walter, I'm sure you figure that giving us a bunch of old bread and rolls and cakes doesn't matter much, but let me tell you. It mattered to Maria. It mattered to that one."

## Things to think about . . .

*Most people think like the young jogger on the beach. They don't think the good they do will matter very much, so why bother? "There are so many hungry people in the world, I can't feed them all. There are so many scared people in the world, I can't comfort them all. So what I do just doesn't matter." But what the old man on the beach knew and what the starfish knew and what Maria knew is that the good things you do* always *matter to someone. Maybe it is a needy person or a needy dog or a needy starfish, but the good you do always matters.*

*It's hard knowing that no matter what you do to*

*make the world a better place, things will look almost exactly the same when you go to sleep as they looked when you woke up. What you need to do is think small. Focus on the one person you can help today. In fact, that's a good thing to think about every night before you go to sleep. Ask yourself before your eyes close, "Did I do something that mattered to someone today?" Did you hug your parents? Did you say something nice to somebody at school? Did you share your toys or your food? If you make a difference to just one person today, then you make a difference to the whole wide world. That is how the world changes—one starfish, one person, one good deed at a time. So get going . . . tomorrow the beach will be full of starfish waiting to be saved.*

# 10

## Stump the Boss:

### Why doesn't God stop the bad things?

"Today we're going to play a game," said Gabe.

"Cool," said Mikey. "I love a good game."

"This one is called Stump the Boss," explained Gabe. "Obviously the Boss is God, and the game is kind of like a quiz show. The point of the game is to ask God a question that God can't answer. So start thinking about what you would ask God."

Later that day Gabe took Mikey down to earth.

They first went to Ground Zero to comfort some people whose friends, or fathers or mothers, or brothers or sisters, or sons or daughters, or grandpas or grandmas, died during the attack on America on September 11.

"Why didn't God stop this?" asked Mikey.

Gabe didn't say anything. Instead they flew off to visit starving children in Africa, who were caught up in war in their country and couldn't get away. They looked like little living skeletons. Many of them were about to die.

"Why didn't God stop this?" asked Mikey.

Again Gabe said nothing. They then visited some prisoners in China who were locked up just because they were Christians in a country where some people aren't allowed to worship God in their own way. Some of the prisoners were about to be taken out and killed.

"Why didn't God stop this?" asked Mikey.

Gabe didn't answer.

"I can't take this anymore!" Mikey finally screamed. "I don't understand it. Why does God allow *so much* evil into the world? God could have allowed just a *little* evil, just enough to show people what not to do, but no, God has let *great big gobs of evil* into the world. God has put *piles of evil, oceans of evil, tons of evil* into the world, and that evil is so . . . *evil* that it makes life on earth miserable for lots of people who didn't do anything to anybody!"

"Didn't anyone ever teach you about the Freedom Rule?" Gabe asked.

"No," Mikey answered sheepishly.

"You were out practicing your loop the loops with your new wings, weren't you?"

"Yup, but I don't think anything they could teach me in Heaven would help me understand why there is so much evil down here," said Mikey.

Gabe sat Mikey down and said, "You can never understand people, or evil, or God, or anything until you understand the Freedom Rule."

"What is the Freedom Rule?" asked Mikey.

"God gave people something called free will," said Gabe. "Free will means that every person gets to decide what he or she will do. God can try to *teach* people the right thing to do, but God can't *make* them do the right thing. They have to use their free will to *decide* to do the right thing.

People are free to decide to do good, or they are free to decide to do bad. God will not stop them from doing either."

"I just don't understand!" yelled Mikey.

Gabe answered patiently, "If God did stop people every time they were about to make a bad choice, then they wouldn't really be free. That's the Freedom Rule, and it is a big rule here on earth. It's because people have free will that evil is possible. Unfortunately sometimes people use their free will to make really bad choices."

"What a stupid rule!" Mikey screamed. "Why couldn't God just take away the Freedom Rule and make people make good choices all the time? The world would be a much better place."

"God could have done that," said Gabe. "God could have made people with no free will and no choices. But God created people to understand the difference between good and evil, between right and wrong, and gave them the freedom to choose the good over the bad."

Mikey was still not satisfied. "But why let people be free when they are just going to keep making bad choices?"

Gabe took a while before answering Mikey with just one word: "Love!"

"Huh?" said Mikey.

"Yes, love is the reason for the Freedom Rule. You see, God wants people not just to obey God but to love God. Love is a feeling that a person must give freely. You can't make somebody love you. You can't order people to love you. They have to *decide* to love you, and if they are not free to decide, they are not free to love. That's the reason God made people free."

"I think I'm starting to understand," said Mikey. "All I can figure is that there is one thing God can't do."

"And what's that?" asked Gabe.

"God can't be stumped," said Mikey. "After all, when you think about it, God knows everything and made everything, and is everywhere and can do anything, anytime, anywhere, anyhow. But because God loves people, God gives them the freedom to make choices. God's unstumpable!"

Gabe smiled at Mikey. "Congratulations, little angel. You won Stump the Boss."

## Things to think about . . .

*If we think it's hard to be a human being, imagine what it must be like to be God. God can hope we will make the right choices with our freedom but can't know for sure.*

*It's kind of the same thing for your parents. They give you freedom and raise you with love, but they can't know for sure if you will take their good advice and do the right thing. Being free is a big responsibility, and it takes time to learn how to make good choices and stay away from bad ones.*

*Mikey saw how bad stuff comes into the world through people's freedom to do terrible things. God must really believe in us a lot to give us freedom. And we wouldn't want it any other way. Even if we don't always use that freedom right, being free is God's greatest gift to us. It's how we get to choose the kind of lives we will live, who we will love, and what we will do next. It's how we know that God loves us. But still, it must be hard to be God and to have to see all the ways we mess up the earth and one another. It's hard to be a human being, but it must be way harder to be God.*

# 11

## Alfie the Atheist:

*Do I have to believe in God to be good?*

One of Gabe's favorite lessons for Mikey was a game Mikey called Follow That Person. Gabe would send Mikey to earth to follow a certain person around for a while and then come back and tell Gabe what he had learned.

One day Gabe said to Mikey, "Follow Alfie."

"Who's Alfie?" Mikey asked.

"He is a boy who lives near Chicago in a white

house with a mom and dad and baby sister and a dog named Trotsky. Bring a video camera so that you can take pictures. I like pictures."

"Okay," said Mikey as he grabbed an invisible angel high-tech video camera and dove down to earth.

Gabe didn't hear a thing from Mikey. He didn't come by. He didn't return his angel camera. He was nowhere to be found. Then, just as Gabe was about to go look for him, Mikey showed up, holding his camera with his head down.

"What's wrong? Where have you been? I was worried about you."

Mikey shuffled his feet and said quietly, "I didn't come around because I didn't want to talk to you. I didn't want to report about Alfie."

"Why? Wasn't he a good boy? I heard he was a very good boy."

"No," said Mikey, "you don't understand. There is *nothing* wrong with this kid at all. In fact, Alfie is the best, kindest, most wonderful human being I have ever seen. Let's go to the videotape and I will show you."

Mikey put a cassette into a machine and showed

it on a white cloud. There was a young boy sitting with a younger girl in a wheelchair. She was laughing at something funny he had just said.

"Alfie sits with that girl every morning while she waits for her bus so that her mom can get to work on time," Mikey explained to Gabe. Next Mikey showed a tape of Alfie playing baseball after school. Alfie walked over to a boy who had not been picked for any team and said, "Hey, would you like to play on my team?" Mikey then showed a tape of Alfie eating lunch at school, where he was surrounded by many friends. There was a boy eating alone. Alfie walked over to him and said, "Hey, Billy, why don't you come over and eat lunch with us?"

After seeing that tape, Gabe just smiled and said, "I know. He is special."

"No, you don't understand, Gabe, he is more than special. He is more than a very, very good person. I never saw him cheat on a test, or lie, or say anything bad about anybody else. He is never jealous of what other kids have, even though his family doesn't have a lot of money. When he goes to get an ice cream cone at Snouder's Ice Cream

Parlor, he always puts some money in the charity can to help feed stray dogs. On the weekends he goes to an old age home and reads books to the old people, and he calls his grandma every week to tell her that he loves her. I'm telling you, this kid Alfie is really something special. He's like a little saint. He's even better than some angels I know! I began to call him Saint Alfie."

"Am I missing something, then?" asked Gabe. "What's the problem?"

"The problem is that Alfie is an atheist. Alfie doesn't believe in God!"

"Really?" said Gabe.

"Yes, really!" said Mikey. "Look, here is a tape of Alfie talking to his teacher after class." Mikey started the tape. Alfie was erasing the blackboard for his English teacher, Ms. Vanderschmeck.

"Merry Christmas, Alfie," she said to him.

Alfie said, "Oh, thank you, Ms. Vanderschmeck, but we don't have Christmas in my house. I'm not Christian."

"I'm sorry, Alfie," she apologized. "Then I guess it's Happy Hanukkah to you?"

"No," Alfie said to her, "I don't celebrate

Hanukkah, either. I'm not Jewish."

"Then, Alfie, is it *Ramadan Mubarak*, Happy Ramadan?"

"Nope. I'm not a Muslim. I'm not a Hindu. I'm not a Buddhist. I'm not anything. I'm just a human being. I'm just an Alfie. That's what my mom and dad keep telling me. They didn't raise me up to be part of any religion. They said that if anybody asks, I should just say that I am a human being and that's enough. Sometimes I wish I was a part of some religion, because religions have nice holidays, and on some of them you get presents and you sing nice songs, but I guess just being a human being is good enough for me."

"Being a person as nice as you, Alfie, is quite good enough," said Ms. Vanderschmeck. "How about this, Alfie?" she said. "Let me be the first to wish you a Very Happy Winter-Spring-Summer-Fall."

Alfie smiled. "Thanks, Ms. Vanderschmeck, and let me wish a Very Happy Winter-Spring-Summer-Fall to you, too."

Then a bunch of students came into Ms.

Vanderschmeck's class. Alfie walked up to each of them and smiled and wished each one a Very Happy Winter-Spring-Summer-Fall. They all looked a little confused, but since it was Alfie nobody minded, and pretty soon everybody in the school was wishing everybody else a Very Happy Winter-Spring-Summer-Fall.

Then Mikey stopped the tape and said to Gabe, "I thought you had to believe in God to be good. I had no idea that a person who does not believe in God could be so good. Everyone in Heaven believes in God, and everyone in Heaven is good."

"Yes, but that's because we are near God every day and we see God every day. Many of the people up here did not believe in God until they got here. And that's why I sent you to follow Alfie. I wanted you to learn that doing the right thing is more important than believing the right thing. There are lots of people who don't believe in God who are very good, and there are lots of people who say they believe in God but who do terrible things. It's the doing that counts. It's the good that counts."

Mikey thanked Gabe for explaining everything.

He then flew down to earth, where he found Alfie and whispered in his ear, "A Very Happy Winter-Spring-Summer-Fall to you, Alfie."

## Things to think about . . .

*Mikey learned an important lesson by following Alfie around:* <u>What you do is way more important than what you believe</u>. *How you live your life is the only way to really check up on what you believe. If you say you believe that cheating is wrong, but then you actually cheat, your belief about not cheating just isn't real. If you say you believe in helping people, but you never really help anybody, then you don't really believe what you say you believe. It's simple. The only way to know what someone* <u>really</u> *believes is to see what that person* <u>does</u>.

*Doing good things is the best way for people with different beliefs to get along together. If you believe that Jesus was the Son of God, but someone in your class at school does not believe that Jesus was the Son of God, that difference of belief might keep you from becoming friends or from doing good things together. There's no need for that to happen. The rescue workers who saved people after* the attack on America on September 11 never asked the people they saved what they believed. They just tried to save people who needed to be saved. When there are so many people who need help in our world, it seems stupid for the rest of us to sit around arguing about who has the best beliefs. People will do good things together even if they don't believe the same things.

It's fine to believe that your beliefs are true and right, but it's important to respect other people's beliefs, too. It's kind of like believing that your parents are the best mom and dad in the whole wide world. It's okay to believe that, as long as you know that there are lots of other really great moms and dads besides yours. It's the same with religions. There are lots of good beliefs and good religions. They are all different and good in their own ways. So we should all try to learn from every person and from every faith and from every belief. It all comes down to this: _A world where everybody believed what you believe would be good, but a world where everybody acted like Alfie would be even better_.

# 12

## Mud:

### Does God still make miracles?

"I never saw one," said Mikey.

"One what?" asked Gabe.

"One miracle. I have never seen a miracle. It's not that I'm complaining or anything. I don't *need* to see a miracle. I just thought it might be cool. Gabe, you got to see Noah's ark and the burning bush, and you got to see the big miracle of the splitting of the Red Sea. I've never seen anything like that!"

"Sounds to me like you *are* complaining," said Gabe.

"Well, maybe just a little. What I don't under-stand is why God doesn't make more miracles. If God would just do miracles, lots and lots of people would believe in God right away."

"Oh yeah? Come with me. I have something to show you." Then Gabe held Mikey's hand and flew with him into a cloud. Suddenly Gabe and Mikey were standing underwater on the bottom of some big sea with fish swimming through the feathers on their wings and through their halos.

"Glurb! Glurb!" said Mikey.

"Glurb," said Gabe.

"GLURB!" said Mikey.

Just then Gabe and Mikey broke through the water and found themselves in the air, with one big wall of water on one side and one big wall of water on the other side and a hallway of air right through the middle of the sea. People and animals were walking between the walls of water. Gabe said in a proud voice, "Welcome to one of God's biggest miracles, Mikey. We are right in the middle of the splitting of the Red Sea."

"*Amazing!*" said Mikey. "How did we go back in time? How did we get here? What's happening?"

"You see, we angels can go back in time as far as we want and whenever we want. We just can't go forward into the future even for one second because nobody, not even God, knows what the future will be," Gabe explained.

"Anyway, you wanted to see a real miracle, so here we are in the Red Sea. These are the children of Israel. Moses is up there in front. They were slaves in Egypt for four hundred years, but today God is taking all of them out of Egypt. We are in the middle of the Red Sea, which God split so that they could get across before the army of Pharaoh catches up to them."

"This is amazing," said Mikey. "I've never been in the middle of a miracle before. I always wondered what it would be like to see one of God's big miracles up close."

"Go look and just listen to them."

Mikey saw two men ahead of him walking

through the sea and looking down. He heard one of them say, "I can't believe all this mud and fog. All I see is mud and fog, mud and fog. What a mess!"

A woman said, "This mud is awful! I'll never be able to get it out of my clothes. I can't believe Moses brought us through this mud. Where are we, anyway?"

"You are in the middle of a miracle!" Mikey shouted at the people. "Look up! Look up at the walls of water! Why can't you see? You are in the middle of the Red Sea!"

"They can't hear you," said Gabe with a sad smile. "You know people can't usually hear angels. We have to help them in other ways."

"Why don't they see the miracle that is all around them? All they see is the mud."

"That's right. These people are in the middle of the biggest miracle God ever did, and all they see is mud and fog. Even this miracle didn't make them believe in God, because they never looked up!"

"That is very sad. Even a big miracle doesn't work on everyone. Let's go home."

Then in a whoosh Gabe and Mikey were back,

but they were not back in Heaven. They were in a field of flowers where a little girl was lying on her stomach looking at one of the flowers.

"What's this?" asked Mikey.

"Just listen to her," said Gabe.

"Dear God, my name is Holly, which you probably know already. I just wanted you to know that these flowers are your best miracle. They are so beautiful, and they open at just the right time in the spring every year. I know you make lots of good things and many miracles, but I wanted to thank you for these flowers today. They may not be your best miracle to everyone, but they are your best miracle for me. Thank you. Oh, and God, if you could tell my big brother not to play his loud music tonight I would appreciate it. I have a big spelling test tomorrow and I need to study."

"You see, Mikey," said Gabe with a big smile, "what makes a person find God is not the miracle but the person."

"I understand," said Mikey, smiling back. "She didn't need a big fancy miracle to find God because she was already looking up."

**Things to think about . . .**

*There are zillions of miracles all over the earth that people would see if they just looked for them. The way our bodies work is a miracle. The way the planets move around and don't crash into one another is a miracle. Babies are miracles. The way people write songs and paint pictures is a miracle. The way people who have not been loved enough are still able to love someone else is a miracle. When people don't have much, but they give some of their stuff to other people who have even less, that's a miracle. When people heal after somebody they love has died, that's a miracle, too. A miracle is something God puts in the world to help us, and there are zillions of miracles to see. People who never expect to see a miracle will never see one, but people who are ready to see God's work in our world see miracles all the time. Look around! How many miracles can you count today?*

# 13

## Just Being There:

### *What should I say to a sad friend?*

"Where's Gabe?" Mikey asked his friend Raziel.

"He's not here today. He's a bit under the weather."

"Why?" asked Mikey. "Gabe is always here. What happened?"

"He just lost one of his favorite people," Raziel said sadly. "He's pretty broken up about it."

"You mean he can't find someone?"

"No, silly, a person he was watching over just died. She lived to be a hundred years old, and she died last night."

"Oh," said Mikey.

"A bunch of us are going over to Gabe's cloud now. You want to come?"

"Absolutely." Raziel and Mikey and Uziel and Wilhelmina flew over to the cloud, where they found Gabe. He looked pretty sad.

"Thank you for coming over. It's good to see you all."

"What was her name, Gabe?" asked Mikey.

"Her name was Dora. She was nice to everybody and never said a mean word about people, even the people who hurt her. She raised four wonderful children, and they had children, and those children had children. But she was old, and last year she fell and broke her hip. After that she was never the same. She died last night. This morning I took her to meet the souls of the people in her family who died before her. They were happy to see her, but everybody on earth is sad. I am sad, too—because there just aren't many people like Dora, and I know her family will miss her," Gabe said.

Raziel came over to Gabe and said, "Gabe, why are you sad? You know that she will be happier here in Heaven. She is with her family, and she will be near God. Life on earth can be so hard and full of bad stuff. Heaven is better, and she is in a better place now. You should not be sad, because Dora is in a better place now and forever."

Gabe said nothing.

Wilhelmina then came over to Gabe and said, "Gabe, you shouldn't be sad. Dora lived a very, very long life. There's nothing to be sad about at all. She lived long and had a big family and children and grandchildren and even some great-grandchildren. Who cares if she died at a hundred years old? This was an *old* woman. Most people never get to live to be even close to a hundred years old. She was lucky to live so long. You shouldn't be so sad. If life was a game, Dora would be one of the winners. Cheer up!"

Gabe said nothing.

Uziel then said, "Yeah, that's right, Gabe. Hey,

nobody's perfect. I bet there were some bad things Dora did sometime in her life. You are letting her off the hook. I'm sure she was a nice lady, but she wasn't as good as we are. She wasn't an angel. She wasn't perfect. Nobody is perfect. Every person does *something* bad."

Gabe said nothing.

Mikey didn't say a word. He just sat next to Gabe with his head in his hands, too. He just sat next to his teacher in silence.

After a while Raziel and Uziel left, but before they did, Raziel said, "Remember, Gabe, she is in a better place now."

Then Wilhelmina left, but before she left, she said, "Remember, Gabe, she won the game of life."

Mikey just sat there next to Gabe, saying nothing. After a long time passed, Mikey said to Gabe, "I'm sorry about Dora. Can I do anything for you?"

Gabe looked up and smiled at Mikey. "You already brought me what I needed the most."

Mikey looked confused. "I don't understand."

Gabe said, "All the other angels spoke to me, but you said nothing the whole time. Why? Why didn't you say anything to me?"

"I'm sorry, Gabe. I'm very sorry. I didn't say anything because I didn't know what to say. I just wanted to be here with you because I love you and you are my teacher. I know you are sad, but I don't know how to make your sadness go away. I'm sorry. Maybe when I get to be—"

"Stop!" Gabe interrupted Mikey and gave him a big hug. "Stop, my little angel. You were the only one of all the angels who really helped me. All of them tried to explain away my sadness. They gave me reasons why Dora's death was okay. I more than anyone know everything is all right for her now, and I know that everything will be all right for her family, but I am still sad to see a good person like her die. I didn't need explanations. I didn't need words. I just needed someone to be there. I needed love. You brought me exactly what I needed. Thank you."

"Gabe, I brought you love and no words because that's all I have."

Gabe hugged Mikey again and said, "You are wise. Mikey, I think you're ready to become a guardian angel . . . unless you still want to quit."

"No, no, I don't want to quit! This is so exciting, I don't even know what to say," Mikey exclaimed.

"Sometimes it's better not to say anything. You know that, Mikey. And that," said Gabe proudly, "is why you will soon be ready."

**Things to think about . . .**

*One thing is for sure. You are going to have days when a friend is really sad. On those days, sometimes words may not be what your friend needs. In fact, usually words are <u>not</u> what people need to feel better. Simply being there with your sad friend might actually be what he or she needs. The same goes for you, too. When you have sad days, being around people who love you might be exactly what you need.*

*Life and its sad parts can't really be explained. You just need to live through them and find the hope and courage to go on with your life. Knowing that you are loved and having those who love you near—even if they don't say anything—is the best medicine for sadness. It doesn't always make sadness go away, but it does make the sadness less painful. Just being there is the best gift you can give and the best gift you can get.*

*There are times when words are good but hugs are better. Lots of people can bring words into this world, but there aren't enough people who can bring love . . . and you don't even have to say a word!*

# 14

## And God Cried, Too:

### Is God ever sad?

"Molly needs you," Gabe said to Mikey.

"Who is Molly?" Mikey asked.

"She is a seven-year-old girl who is having a hard time right now. Her dad was a firefighter who was killed in the terrible attack on America on September 11. She is still very sad. That's why she needs you . . . and who knows, you just might learn something very important."

"Like what?"

"You'll see. But in the meantime, I want you to help Molly feel better."

"I'll try, but I'm not sure I know what to do."

"You will be just fine. Follow your heart."

"Where is Molly now?" Mikey asked.

"Come. I will take you to her."

Gabe and Mikey found Molly playing with some little wooden toy logs that kids use to build log cabins. Molly was talking to her dog, Topper, who was lying next to her on the rug in her bedroom.

She was busy building a house with the logs when she said to Topper, "I miss my dad so much. He was trying to save people from a big burning building, and even though he knew it was very dangerous, he went into the building anyway. A lady even called my mom and told her that my dad had saved her life and then gone back into the building to save other people, but the building crashed down on him."

She stopped talking and just put her head in her hands and started to cry.

It was a deep but quiet cry. It was the kind of cry

that shakes your whole body. After a while she dried her eyes on her sleeve and took up another little wooden log and put it on one of the walls. She had four walls almost built, and soon she would be ready to put the green roof on the log cabin and a little plastic chimney on top of the roof.

She said, "This house is for my dad. Of course, it's too small to fit my whole daddy, but my mom says that it's just his soul that went to Heaven. So I figure his soul is smaller and would maybe fit. And anyway, I can't build anything bigger because I only have these little logs."

"What do I do?" Mikey asked Gabe. "This is so sad."

"You must try to figure it out," said Gabe as he flew off, leaving Mikey alone in the room with Molly and Topper.

"Molly! It's lunchtime," shouted her mother from the kitchen. "I made your favorite, macaroni and cheese."

Molly put down the little log she was holding and walked downstairs. Topper knew the word *cheese*, and since cheese was his favorite thing in the whole wide world, he ran downstairs ahead of

Molly and began sniffing around for anything that might have fallen on the floor.

Molly returned to her room after lunch and started working on her log cabin again. Within no time, all four walls of the log cabin were finished, and the green roof was finished, and even the little plastic chimney was put in just the right place on top of the roof. "I hope my dad likes the log cabin. I just wish I knew that he was okay and that he really is in Heaven," she said softly to Topper, who had followed her back upstairs.

In a gentle voice Mikey said to Molly, "Your dad *is* in Heaven. He will watch over you and protect you and love you . . . and so will I."

Molly was sitting completely still on the floor when her mom came up the stairs and into Molly's room.

"Are you okay, honey?"

Molly hugged her mom hard and said with tears in her eyes, "You know what, Mom? I'm okay. I really miss Daddy, but I know that he is watching over me. He will love me forever. I am still sad and miss him so much, but I am okay."

Molly and her mom were hugging each other

hard and crying hard. A tear from Molly fell onto the green roof of the little log cabin with the plastic chimney. A tear from her mother fell onto the roof as well.

On the way back to Heaven, Gabe said, "You are going to be a great guardian angel someday, Mikey. You were wonderful with Molly."

"Thanks, Gabe. There is just one thing. . . ."

"What's that?"

"Well, I saw three tearstains on the green roof of the little log cabin. Molly cried, and her mother cried. But who cried the third tear?"

"You know the answer, Mikey. Feel it in your heart," answered Gabe.

Mikey stopped. Suddenly he realized why Gabe had brought him to Molly. Through her, he had just learned his most important lesson.

As he looked over at Gabe, Mikey whispered softly, "Molly cried, her mother cried . . . and God cried, too."

**Things to think about . . .**

*God can't <u>change</u> what you feel, but God can <u>feel</u> what you feel. When you're happy, God is happy;*

when you're sad, God is sad. It's great to know that however you feel, you don't have to feel that way alone.

When somebody you love dies, there's no question, it's really sad. But believe it or not, there is actually one good thing about feeling sad. Your sadness is proof that you really loved that person. Feeling sad means that you gave your love out to somebody else. Think of it this way. Your sadness is like a love thermometer. The more you love someone, the sadder you'll be when that person dies. And when you really give out your love, the sadness can really hurt. But that kind of hurt should make you feel proud. It proves that you gave your whole heart to someone else.

When somebody you love dies, people may say to you, "Everything will be okay." What they really mean is that things will be okay in a new way. The person who died won't be in your life in the same way ever again. But your life will go on. Your love for the person who died, and his or her love for you, will never leave you. You can't live with that person anymore, but you can live with the memory of his or her love. That's what will make your life *okay in a new way. Death doesn't make our lives terrible forever. Death just makes our lives terrible for a while. Then life is okay again, but in new ways that we learn to accept.*

*What everybody can be sure of is that love makes you feel better. Love is the best thing we get, and the best thing we give, and the only thing that never ever dies.*

*Just remember this: every time you cry . . . God is crying, too.*

# 15

## The Thunder Test:

*What can I do when I'm afraid?*

"What now?" asked Mikey with great excitement. He had just learned that he was actually about to become a guardian angel.

Gabe said with a smile, "You just need to go to God."

"Great. Where do I find God?"

"Right through there," said Gabe. He was

pointing to a big, black cloud with lightning and thunder coming from it.

"No way! Nope! Sorry! I can't go there. I'm afraid of thunder and lightning and big black clouds where everything goes *boom crackle boom*! Gabe, I can't go that way. I'm too afraid."

"Mikey, you have to go through the thunder-cloud."

"You mean every guardian-angel-in-training has to fly through a thundercloud?"

"No, only you. Other angels have to face what-ever they fear the most. You can't be a guardian angel until you face your biggest fears and get through them somehow," said Gabe.

"What did you have to do?" Mikey asked.

"I had to jump into a deep, dark ocean and find God there," said Gabe, shaking a bit. "It was cold and dark. It was the hardest thing I ever had to do. But I got through it and so will you. I believe in you, Mikey. You will be okay. Just close your eyes, keep going forward, and don't look back."

"I can't. I can't fly through the thundercloud. I'm sorry, Gabe, I can't do it. I'll take the deep ocean any day. I like water. I just hate thunder."

"You can do it, Mikey. You can find your way to God through that cloud. Just fly forward and don't give up." Gabe gave Mikey a pat on the back and gently pushed him right into the thunder-cloud.

Mikey flew into the cloud with his eyes closed tightly and prayed softly. Then *Boom! Crash! Boom!* Mikey was in the middle of terrible thunder and lightning. The wind tossed him around and around and up and down and sideways and backward. He didn't even know if he was still flying forward. He was soaked by the rain and his wings were tired. As he felt himself sinking, Mikey said a prayer. "Oh, God, I am so scared. Please find me. Please save me. I am just one little angel, and this cloud is so big and dark and scary."

"I am always with you," came a voice from the middle of the storm.

"Who is that?" asked Mikey.

"I am watching over you," said the voice. "You have nothing to be afraid of. I am with you on stormy days and on sunny days. On days when sadness is everywhere and on days when happiness is everywhere, I am with you."

Mikey realized it was God's voice. "Always?" he asked.

"Always," answered God. Then Mikey felt the wind stop. Just as suddenly the thunder and lightning stopped. Mikey felt a feeling that he had never felt before. It was kind of like the way he loved his teacher, Gabe, and kind of like the way he loved his friends, and kind of like the way he loved the people he met on earth who were trying to do good things. But this feeling was deeper and stronger. Then Mikey opened his eyes and . . . he was home, on his own cloud, and Gabe and all his friends were there. They were cheering for him and patting him on the back. "Hooray for Angel Mikey! Hooray!"

Gabe came over to Mikey and gave him a big hug. "I knew you would make it, my little angel. I knew you would become a guardian angel someday. God bless you!"

Mikey hugged Gabe back and said, "God already blessed me way before today. God blessed me the day God sent you to be my teacher. Thank you, Gabe, for not letting me give up, and God bless *you!*"

"Let's go celebrate," Gabe said to Mikey. Then the teacher and his student looped the loop all over Heaven.

**Things to think about . . .**

*Everybody is afraid of something. What are you afraid of?*

*Talking about what scares you with the people who love you will help you get rid of your fears. Also it helps to do what Gabe told Mikey to do. Just close your eyes and keep flying forward. Remember that what God told Mikey is true for all of us.*

*God is with us always and everywhere. Maybe God sends angels to keep track of us and protect us, or maybe God does it without angels, but somehow, in some way, we are not alone. Even when people don't love us, God does. Even when people hurt us, God doesn't, and even when nobody seems to believe in us, God does.*

*It doesn't matter if you don't believe in angels. What does matter is that you believe that you are not alone. What does matter is that you know that you are loved by God!*